EXTRAORDINARY EPIPHANIES OF A KING

Inspired Poetry & Prose
Messages of Life

King Andre' Teasdell

DEDICATION

When I think of dedication, I think of Love...

When I think of Love, I think of 'you' as Love, because 'you' were made by Love, for love, to love, as Love!

You know, that is the "ALL" of what GOD is! The infinite, unlimited expanse of everything ... Yes, EVERYTHING!

If you are not aware of this thought as "True," then, you must come to expand your relationship with the "One" that created you, in dedication of love, and the love of all created.

But, many have yet to reach that level of understanding; and unfortunately, there are many who will never reach!

So, I dedicate this, to everyone who reached me, spoke with me, and touched me in love!

You "Already" Know!

Namaste'

CONTENTS

TABLE OF RECALL

1. **ESCHEW NOT** (FALL 2004) – The mystery of meeting others, often leaves lasting impressions. Transporting clients and having good conversations can inspire the mind into deeper thought than when traveling alone. We spoke and identified that the only constant in the realm of human existence is *CHANGE*. As I pondered upon this philosophical theory, I stumbled upon these words emanating from within my soul. What amazed me most is I didn't know the meaning of the word 'eschew'. Wow, talk about your *"Living Thought"*! I prepared my first draft of this which is written herein because I remember my client saying, "The things that are real seem to forever exist, where the things that are less real quickly seem to fade."

2. **CAN YOU SAY GOODBYE TO A DEAD MAN** (FALL 2004) – My earthly Father, Neahmiah Teasdell, died October 14, 2000. His remains lie in the Garrison Forest Veteran Cemetery in Maryland. Although the scripture says, "To be absent from the body is to be present with the Lord," I still can't break the habit of talking with him or expecting

him to walk through the door, and yet, my eyes still water sometimes when I think about him. So why visit a grave where only what remains behind resides? Maybe, deep within myself, I know there is more in store.

3. **ONCE WROTE** (Epiphany Sunday, Jan. 8, 2006) – It was the 3rd Anniversary evening service celebration at the Greater Victory and Deliverance Church of Jesus Christ, and I had no idea that the young man I had trained in emergency medical care, about 15 years prior, would be speaking of me from the pulpit. This Pastor couldn't refrain from mentioning his experience under my tutelage. He recalled the words from the written performance evaluation I had given him that said, "We are all better learned when we are exposed to the field in which we are to learn." My epiphany taught me that your influence upon another may one day influence you in return.

4. **BEWARE OF THE VESTIBULE** (1999) – Many childhood discoveries were unmasked in the vestibule. Many of these discoveries were not innocent by any means. It was sometimes known as the secret place of the girls, and I recall a walking salesman or insurance agent,

who was also known to do magic. One day, we asked him if he could make people disappear. Then, either my sister or one of her friends went into the vestibule. Just like they do on television, we didn't see her again until he brought her back. When we asked her what happened, she said she could hear us but only saw darkness.

5. **A LITTLE BIT OF LIFE IS NEVER ENOUGH** (1997) – "Life without love ain't worth living" is a lie straight from the devil. Without love, life would have never come to be. In 1997, I was catching all kinds of hell because my life plans were coming apart at the seams. I wrongfully equated the love I felt for my spouse, at the time, in higher regard than the love and devotion I should have had towards God. My spiritual perception of life had become twisted. I began to press my relationship for greater love, and had disconnected myself from the understanding that only God is the source of real love. All true love is nourished by His presiding Love. It is God who is the eternal supply that never runs dry because love is the substance of the life force we cannot see.

6. **SHADOWS OF** (1989) – Reflecting upon my life and all that has been. What is becoming of me? Time does not stop, and all that has been are only shadows of what used to be. I used to be a bachelor just 3 years ago. Now, I am married with a new baby, all my friends of before are gone, and all my relationships with everything are different. I pray I have not chosen the counterfeit over that which is real.

7. **NO ONE** (2005) – The experiences of what has become of me after going through a marriage that is no more, is just one of the things that has led me to knowing that people can be heartless and cruel. But, no matter what happens to you individually, somebody somewhere will always be affected. Each person must have their own unique experiences to understand that experiences are as different as each new snowflake or like fingerprints. No two are exactly the same, yet, we all are of one origin and no one can live life unto himself. Therefore, no one should hurt alone because in living, hurt is easier to bare when you know that someone is there who cares. My hurt caused me to believe that love was not mine to have until a friend said straight up, "This living ain't heaven because

it's designed to bring you pain, so suck it up and claim your strength, until you get where you need to be."

8. **THE ACCUSER** (2004) – I cannot stand having to defend myself of any accusation of a wrong that I know I did not commit. That's like a challenge to my integrity. Don't get me wrong, I ain't a saint, but I have enough to stand accused of without being accused of that which I did not do. Personally, that's how I feel about it, but who doesn't stand accused of something, somewhere at sometime in their life, except the ultimate sin offering? Still, we will constantly hear, "It's all your fault," or "Why don't you bear your own burdens?" But, I have this one question, "Who is it that chooses to build you up only to watch you fall and tear you down?"

9. **PAID ATTENTION** (2005) – It took me some time to recognize the benefits of my pain, but during the hurt, it seems the pain is the only thing to think about. But you mustn't get stuck in that moment of your living because whatever you go through is your cost. So, don't get overtaxed because you couldn't move on. Your ticket into your tomorrow is learning when to leave the

past behind. Therefore, do not neglect your experiences, nor let your lessons be stolen. Also, never let the agony of your pain be your primary focus when recognizing *our lessons of life is where we earn the Gold.*

10. **DONE** (1989) – It's that 'old paper bag syndrome' taking its stand once again. No longer am I seen as valued and cherished like before, and I can't figure out why. This relationship is really turning hostile. Every time I strive to make her happy, it's like a bomb blows up in my face. My world is crumbling and slipping through my hands, as if my feelings no longer matter, as if I no longer exist.

11. **LINES** (2004) – Relationships can only begin to form if we cross the lines that keep us separated from the love of one to another, be it family, friend, or foe. Yes, it's true that boundaries do have reasons for existence; but when the purpose of the lines is no longer of benefit, then why should anyone be locked out of their chosen destiny? Imaginary barriers divide nothing when everything is relative.

12. **SHORT LIVED** (1999) – As we are of a living existence, we find that there are

many things that do not live a long life. The young die young and the old die old, but what of the life of a butterfly in comparison to the fly? It's interesting that the life of the butterfly and even the life of the salmon all have their season. They all have their season and use their time wisely to be an accomplished being, each bringing forth its fruit. However, do all humans possess the same spirit of fruitfulness to be a productive part of the whole? Observing nature grows an appreciation of creation.

13. **FAMILY TREES** (FAMULI SEEDS) (1998) – Sometimes I feel that the greatest problem in America stems from the *poison* of misconceptions and prejudices being handed down from generation to generation, without the realization that poison is death to all who drink it. I used the original root word of family to show how things can change over time, and in the roots of families, you can often find that which generates lies against other cultures which will poison generations to come. This is the kind of thinking that is deadly to the unaware. I was almost brought to tears when I watched a news documentary of an Aryan mother's influence upon her children,

against people that they knew nothing about. The children spewed their hate about others, who were not their kind, as if it was the right thing to do. What is it that your family has been feeding on? Is it life or is it death? In keeping our eyes and minds clear of debris and the filth of nonsense, we will better improve our path into a brighter tomorrow, no matter who your Mama is. (Famulus, from Latin meaning servant).

14. **B®OTHER** (2000) – R U listening? Can U here me? It seems kind of misplaced to find letters in place of words or the same sound with a different spelling in a place it shouldn't be. Sometimes that's just what trouble feels like when you're caught up in it, especially when there's no one who seems to understand your "Y". I am one of many who has no blood brother, yet a group called Children and Father's Workforce and Development (CFWD) gave me help when facing the pain of not being family any more. Sometimes, the worst blood amongst family is bad blood that cannot see the good in you. In the CFWD group, I found a whole group of brothers who shared "MA'AT" when I needed someone to share something positive.

15. **WORD-VERB** (2005) – "In the beginning was the Word." For a minute, it sounds kind of crazy to think that a word can be something other than a group of letters together that can form a sound. But, then I thought, *What is life without words?* Just imagine having nothing to form a concept or to link into something. Word is action, word is sound, and sound is energy. Yet, isn't it true that in order for there to be many, there must first be the one, unless you act not upon "The Word"?

16. **CHOICES WE KEEP** (2001) – As a Paramedic, I've seen the after-effects of much violence, murder, and the actions of many against one another. Outside of being a Paramedic, I've seen the attacks, heard the screams, and seen them fall. Imagine trying to tell a shooting victim, who can talk only of retribution, not to make the wrong choice that would only escalate violence to another level. Imagine saving a life that may very well go back out into society with the sole purpose of killing another for revenge. Sometimes it seems that we are unable to turn away from the choices that may only bring the worst of consequences until it becomes too painful to bear. It would seem most logical to aim to make no

more bad decisions, especially when those decisions may lead to death, but, then again, what is logic to the irrational mind?

17. **SHAMEFUL LUST** (2005) – Same sex marriages and civil unions are in the forefront of today's news, yet, what shall the future bring with it when she arrives? I shall not speak to judge another if I can help myself. But, everyone needs to recognize and hear the conclusion of the whole matter, and not only the part that may satisfy a private desire that excludes all other applicable variables. So much debating of whether the rights of civil liberties are being violated, by the government or by society at large, is forever changing. But, what about the never changing laws of God? Do we ignore them because it is more convenient for self satisfaction, or is it that 'man' has concluded that he has the authority to make any law above that which God has already established? Now, how dangerous is that? Please remember, disagreeing does not mean that others do not care, but don't lose your soul behind not being sure!

18. **GROWL** (2005) – "That ain't right!" is what I think of many of the things that

have gone wrong. Sometimes life seems so unfair when I begin to reflect upon the injustices that have happened to me and others. "It makes you want to holler," yet I become so angered until it makes me want to growl. I can find no purposeful logic of injustice toward one another. When observing what's going on, I begin to feel the need for effective action to take its course. Yet, what are the best actions we can take without taking the bite out of our fight against injustice, violence and hate? But, then I think of God's word, "Vengeance is mine; I will repay," saith the Lord. So I've learned to "Let patience have its perfect work!" Still, there is something astir.

19. **MILES TO GO** (2005) – I've been through so many storms in my life and have lost everything I had, except my mind. Loss is one of the most painful experiences of life and yet the clouds never cease to form. You learn better how to deal with life's storms as you grow. The truth is the pain really never goes away. You just learn better how to live because of it. The slate is now clear and any unnecessary burdens would only slow down my progress. But to persevere, well, that's what kings are made of!

20. **DARK SUNSHINE** (Apr. 30, 2000) – In the darkest days of my living, depression overwhelmed me. I became out of sync with the rhythm of what I had planned for my life. My life became shattered. First, my marriage, then my job, and finally, my dreams of becoming something more. It seemed everything in my life was under attack, and I was giving up on myself. I didn't want to be aware anymore of anything. I chose to disappear; but then, an awareness came upon me that all of us are connected. Each of us has a special task that is not to be ignored. Who dares to choose to be the weakest link? "Not I!" Not anymore!

21. **DESIRES OF THE FLESH** (Mar. 24, 1999) – Making $100 in fifteen minutes doesn't seem to be all that bad, but I had chosen to stop strip dancing after I married. Nonetheless, one of my buddies ended up in a bind with no dancers for a prepaid contracted engagement, a bachelorette party. I told my wife about the situation, but she left the final decision of this private party in my lap, along with any consequences that could arise. Unfortunately, I didn't see what she had seen. I only knew I couldn't let my buddy down. Temptation seldom brings

the best results. I had turned back after the performance because I left my music. Upon my return, all the elders had already left, which made the girls feel there were no restraints. I hadn't realized the dangerous impression my performance could leave. They had become wild and hungry for "more," but I knew "The Tempter" couldn't stay. Although, I was confident of not committing any wrong, I couldn't see the actuality of my wife's insecurity. How did my turning back affect my life and what was to come? Yes, I was in the doghouse for the night, and I chose the "blank-blank" company of naked visuals on VHS until I fell asleep. However, instead of waking up to my video player on repeat mode, I awoke to a televangelist sermon about a servant named Lot. His wife was transformed into a pillar of salt because she disobeyed God. She looked back at the place she was told to escape.

22. **HIM** (2005) – Can we focus on what He is doing or, are we too distracted by the others? Who is He? He is the Spirit that transforms our nature into the love it ought to be; and He is the one who is there to help us become all we need to be. During that time, we begin changing our character to become like

Him and more of what He has called us to be. Therefore, do not let the distractions take you away from what you are supposed to be. If you let Him, He is you if, of course, you do not confuse who He is. God appears to be a confusing concept to many people because of a lack of understanding. This requires a great deal of soul searching because our souls didn't just come from out of nowhere. I found, as my purpose, a compelling desire to seek him, especially since I found it hard to see myself when I discovered that it was I, who was blocking the path to understanding.

23. **KING TO THE KING** (2005) – Being named King has been unusually difficult for me. I would have never attempted to take on a responsibility that is not my own, but sometimes the cards of life are dealt long before we begin to perceive our existence. I've struggled most of my life with why I was named King. Then I thought about all He's done for me, the experiences I've survived, how I persevered, and all of my wrongdoings. From this reflection, I discovered that He's never rejected me or withheld his love. I've learned that God rules and I must be obedient to His will, because I don't like

the consequences that disobedience brings. God speaks to each of us about our calling. The key is to be perceptive enough to hear. You see, everything is worth surviving when it's God who is leading you through. I would not have made it this far without Him. Everything wrong can be made right when choosing to be obedient to the truth. Because of this, I am determined to make my mark reaching out to others because it was God who chose to reach down to me.

24. **WE** (2004) – There are 'the others' who would have you believe that God has no Love for you. I beg of you not to accept this lie. 'The others' will be held accountable for what they do against us because Divine justice always prevails. "We are" because we are made to be. What made us is God's love, and nothing shall exclude those of us, who believe based on what we receive, because His *LOVE* is supreme. What makes us different is that we are what they are not.

25. **GOD'S GIFT** (1998) – Working to keep my marriage from crumbling apart was one of my greatest struggles to date. But, I failed miserably and am now separated from what I thought would

last forever. Why did I marry? I married because the gifts of God are love, grace and mercy. These are the things that help keep marriages strong, but I began to notice that the destructive forces against these gifts were taking over because she couldn't see that "Truth" was being ignored.

26. **EYE OF THE MIND** (1998) – A foreboding destructive force has arrived, accusing me falsely, and I could do nothing to make a 'made up mind' see the truth. Where and how are these untruths contrived? Where could they be coming from and how could such things have been thought of me? I'm not a part of this, so I had to ponder in the deepest of thought to discover the "Eye of the mind".

27. **"E" IS THE REALITY** (1992) – Here I am, beginning to spread myself too thin to please. I'm a married man working two jobs and attempting to act as though that's the normal thing to do. It's early morning and cold outside, so I decide it's best to warm-up the car before leaving from work. Running off at the gab, it suddenly dawned on me that I needed to move with a quickness. I then noticed that there was no exhaust coming from the tail pipe of my

car. I must have been a little more than distracted because I forgot that I was running behind schedule yesterday and did not stop to refuel. When there is no gas, "E" ain't no joke.

28. **FREEDOM: WHAT DO YOU MAKE OF IT?** (1997) – I was told of the 'Fedora Bandit,' as my co-workers teased me about how much this nicknamed bank robber looked like me. I thought they were acting silly until my buddy, Reggie, showed me a newspaper clipping. I was so amazed at the resemblance I stayed home until that man was captured rather than go to work. Suddenly, freedom meant so much more, especially mine. My freedom was now 'on the line' because of someone else's actions. I thought to myself, *if I couldn't convince my wife of my faithfulness to her, what would I look like attempting to explain something I didn't do, to a stranger.* So I took the time to review history and embrace how freedom is so very precious. Then I thought how I was within my own cage for fear of mistaken identity. It seems society sometimes looks for any reason to alienate someone or any group if they are selected as someone to point the finger at. Sometimes, it's due to

ignorance of which we can't escape. History and man's behavior against nature speaks for itself. Yet, none should take oppression as a thing to be ignored. History has been known for not keeping the best records, and with these conditions, I sure didn't need to incur a criminal record that was not my own doing. But, the real truth is that life is so much more than what confines us.

29. **MIND, BODY, AND SPIRIT** (2006, revised) – I have always been one who wonders about the working of things, and from these thoughts, many mysteries came forth including a strange confusion about, "What is spirit?" There exists 'The Spirit Divine,' the human spirit, evil spirits, and 'The Great Spirit'. Also, there exists the soul of man. In this passage are the words that helped me better understand and apprehend what seems to be unnecessarily elusive, as I continue through years of thought. But of course, we cannot ignore that the mind, the body and the soul all have their roles as well.

30. **LIVING THROUGH IT** (2003) – Alas, I've been knocked out again, and literally left for dead in the street. The

attempt this time was clear that the attack upon my life was to kill me and destroy whatever purpose there is of my being any good. But again, I didn't die because it wasn't my time. However, I had to make a decision. Was I going to allow myself to remain vulnerable to these blatant attacks toward me and the effects they would have upon my family or was I going to put on the full armor of God? You see, no matter what you may believe, I know that there would be no me without the Grace of Divine Intervention. I've always been a believer, but I've also found it more convenient not to act within the parameters of His Truth in order to have it my way. My ways seem to lead a little more towards death than what I'm ready to accept for now. This is what facilitated my greater awakening, because there's got to be a reason why I lived through it all. Remember, Life is for learning, but don't hinder your own growth through selfishness.

31. **THE IDLE MIND** (2005) – "The idle mind is the devils workshop!" Now, that's the 'sho-nuff' truth! I was listening to my favorite radio program, "The Donnie Simpson Show," when the beloved news anchor, David Haines

was reporting, "D.C.'s crime was on the decline because studies show that programs designed to keep inner city youth busy doing constructive things, have a positive result of less crime and violence." Of course, less sin leads to Godly peace. So, this made me wonder if more than the inner city youth are left idle.

32. **MONSTER INSIDE, MONSTER OUT** (1989) – There are times when anger can get the best of us and in turn, manipulate our emotions to express an attitude that is totally out of character. Behavior of this degree can cause destruction of property and breed feelings that will question the security of your stability in the minds of others. Without self-control, you are liable to tear something up that is not on the schedule. If you're living with that kind of buildup within, then you must find the right way of getting it out, because that kind of buildup does not belong. If you have to flex your testosterone, keep it in the gym.

33. **WE ARE MORE** (1997) – Pronouncing a body 'dead on arrival' is nothing new for a seasoned Paramedic. The paperwork is filled out, left with the next authorized division, and then the

body is picked up by the coroner's office after any investigations. But, it is not in my normal flow to see the same dead person, over 24 hours later, somewhere other than I last remember the body to had been. Being a little shaken by this, I began to think about the soul that takes flight seconds after the last breath when the body should not move again on its own.

34. **SHE** (1999) – I don't let just any woman turn my head, but before me this day stood one woman whom I describe as a 'Beautiful Nubian Princess'. I made sure to tell her because you don't see beauty like that every day. Well, to my amazement, I came to meet this creature of loveliness again and we became friends through friends out of respect for our friends. I discovered that she was intelligent, a poet, and had aspirations and goals. As a result of her social choices, she was willing to exchange money for certain favors. I would never have thought her to be of that character. But, because of her character and others just like her, I learned that God's love is not 'SKIN' deep. Every woman is far more than the fleshly shape that turns the heads of men, and it's high time that both sexes get their heads out of the gutter

and turn them back to the sky.

35. **POET'S TREE** (1995) – When nobody is trying to listen, words are all you have. I sometimes find I am often relieved of stress and aggravation after writing down my thoughts. Some use journals, but I found it easier to write on anything just to let my feelings out instead of letting them stay bottled up inside. I remember climbing trees in my youth to get away from it all. Now that I am older, I'm amazed at how words and phrases seem to take on their own form. But, remember it's from within the acorn that lives the hope of the great oak.

36. **THE FALLING OF THE LEAVES** (Oct. 2004) – We, as people, have so much in common with nature that if we open our eyes and minds, we can begin to see traces of love, unity and togetherness in its character. But, because of our diversities, the intellect of man seems to use our differences as a tool to keep us apart. Yet, those who stand out from among the average person need to stand up for all equality.

37. **REJECTION** (2004) – I had a flashback to the worst part of my life,

but sometimes that's when you're faced with the detour of "NOT RIGHT NOW" instead of a choice. This day's client is at the Pentagon and offers me anything I desire. I thank him, but I chose to wait in the car as his guests shop at the PX. While waiting, I decided that it wouldn't be a bad idea to get a snack. However, instead of a snack, I get to chew on a piece of the past. It was just another taste of a thing called 'rejection'. Have you had any lately?

38. **LET THERE BE PEACE** (Dec. 2005) – The death toll of war causalities are alarming and far too often. Death comes because somebody says, "We are at war!" The Iraqi war, the war on drugs, Gang wars, racial and social injustices as well as domestic violence are out of control. There are also drive-by shootings, intolerance amongst parents at scholastic games, violence in schools, and the list goes on. *The weapons against man has more to do with attitude than Arms*. It is evident that the weapons go far deeper than nuclear. Why is it that we are so concerned about the distractions from what we ought to be? Instead, our souls should be most concerned with *Love MINUS the hurt*.

39. **MAYBE LOVE** (May 2005) – People become so twisted about whether or not love, forgiveness and forgetting can co-exist in the same place. Splitting hairs will not solve the problem of indifference if it makes no difference when all the hairs are gone. People need to wake up and get it together before it's too late. *Patience is a virtue, but don't count on it lasting forever*. I had been blessed to hear an album entitled "Escapology". In one of the songs, artist Robbie Williams mentioned that maybe forgiveness is a place. What if this insight that Robbie and I share is the proper way of viewing LOVE today? So, I suggest that maybe we all rethink this thing about Love and our place in its giving. Thanks, Robbie, for the motivation.

40. **MONKEY ON YOUR BACK** (Aug. 2005) – Over the years, I have been inspired by several artists, starting with Stevie Wonder, Marvin Gaye, Nat King Cole, "Earth, Wind and Fire," Prince, and R. Kelly. But, in the summer of 2005, I couldn't stop playing Robbie Williams' "Escapology." I would never have heard of him if I hadn't found the CD abandoned in the limo. Apparently, it was not happenstance because it sure helped create a fantastic summer.

Robbie's lyrical genius brought inspiration with a simple line, "How did I get caught up with this 'blank, blank' monkey anyhow?" Although we all should accept responsibility for our own actions, it's much easier to blame the "monkey on your back syndrome" instead!

41. **DON'T LET THE DEVIL DRIVE** (Aug. 2004) – Years ago during our community prayer gathering, Joanne introduced a song titled, "Don't Let the Devil Ride." In the song was a line that says, "If you give him an inch, he'll take the mile" and another says, "If you give in to him, he'll take charge over your all." Well, life is full of experiences and I chose once to give up the struggle because it looked like I wasn't going to win. I gave up all of what was left of my responsibilities because, after my emotional trauma, I didn't want to fight anymore. But, my surrender was to the left instead of the right, until I realized that my left was totally wrong and there was nothing right about it. The gathering of these words for this script is sort of like a true story because as a driver, I have discovered if you let the devil's influences manipulate you within, he will run you into the ground. And with evil running wild, the last

thing anyone would want to do is have a real life "Stephen King/Twilight Zone" moment of no return.

42. **A SPARK** (Jan. 2006) – To get going each time the energy of writing starts to power-out, sometimes it takes a 'jump-start'. But, when everything seems dead around you with no sense of motivation, what happens in order to make things start again? What happens if it doesn't? Then, where and what becomes of us, if there is nothing to get our 'engines' going again? I am speculatively speaking, of course!

43. **COME FORTH** (Apr. 2005) – Those of the "Lazarus Syndrome," or maybe those who are the "zombies of life," are walking among us void of the reality that FEAR is a tomb that traps the courage of a man. That DEPRESSION is like a darkness that hides our insecurities and feelings of worthlessness from ourselves. The SHAME is like being covered with something foul, which has an odor quite unpleasant to others, including to the one who feels the shame. Maybe those walking in the shadow of death are not conscious of the truth that these feelings can change for anyone and everyone, who has ever been

afflicted and affected by the poisonous sufferings of foul living. It is of these who have also been blinded by the truth of knowing that it is easier for them to come out of their tombs of disgust, than to be retrieved from out of the depths of its darkness and captivating stench, because not everyone can enter therein and come out unaffected. It's very important for everyone to become aware that every situation can be better resolved when we can clearly separate the difference from the night and day of it, and be freely severed from its clinging forces upon what is left of the consciousness that is not yet dead. You see, all cleansing is easier in the light than in the darkness of blind living.

44. **ROLLED AWAY FROM THE TOMB** (Apr. 2005) – I'm drawing correlations from our own living and the expressions of, "What if we let the 'HE THAT IS IN ME' be revealed as an expression of our awakening?" Here lies another among the writ: Trapped by our own choices, devoid of love, we cannot seem to get out of our conditions, no matter what we try to do. Helpless and imprisoned by these choices, our living begins to strangle the life from us, clawing and fighting

amongst ourselves. We seldom think of what the *power of love* can do. If we can begin adding the power of love, the power of love's determination, and the power that love has to break us out of every situation, it couldn't help but result in positive change. Adding this powerful addition consistently to our every situation by living love, removes all pain, aches, hurts and callousness. What seems to block our development is a kind of mental imprisonment of these things that should have been removed and rolled away a long time ago. A dear friend of mine lost all hope and accepted the doom of her poor choices until she stepped into accepting the love of Jesus by rejecting the lies of Satan. The cost has long been paid, and you can enter into the land of the living by simply removing the stone that holds you unnecessarily within your past.

45. **RESURRECTION** (Apr. 2005) – In the beginning was the Word, yet in today's world, the word appears to be dying. How crazy is that when in nearly every horror movie, the appearance of the dead terror always seems to rise again from what appears to be its end? It's unbelievable to think that today's worldly thinking will give more

expectation to such imaginings than "Christ". Many are still jumping in horror at every scene which inevitably will occur anyway. But, to speak of a truly risen Savior, who has risen because of *Love's power* even over death, is considered quite ludicrous when applying such to an already dying world. Well, it's true that the world is dying, but not the 'Word'; and I am not one who is giving up my choice to life when I am convinced the wrath of God is real enough to know who stays and who goes. I've already taken my chances at choice, and I've made my choice through deductive reasoning. For example, I've tried the rest, but now I know what is best. *Remember, there isn't any forcing in the choosing against the losing.* The real winning team is always recruiting and is never mad at you if you chose the contrary. It's only sad to see you chose to go the way that's not in your best interest because we are the ones who want you to choose the best for you. We don't and can't make any choices for you. Your choices are your responsibility. "Live or Let Die", "Deal or No Deal", it's all left up to you.

46. **I WANT TO BE** (Dec. 2005) – Okay, I get it! Nobody is here to live forever.

That's fine and dandy. But, you know I cannot believe that all we are here for is to turn to dust, be eaten by worms and rot, or witness the consuming wrath of God upon unbelieving people. I cannot accept these consequences as part of my existence, because I know there is so much more…. *It's has to be!* Why is there a need for God? Because, nothing on this side can last as long as eternity and that's where I'm headed. Are you going my way?

47. **LISTEN** (Jan. 2006) – Hey, I do this thing because of the Love of God that is within me. I never thought I'd ever be writing in this format. My thought was of writings for medical journals and my findings of laboratory research to enhance the good of mankind, but, that's where things began to change. The food of mankind can have no worth if man has no body for the soul to come, or to go. Just as with anything, you have to qualify for the next level. Many will not qualify and many are disqualified, but, the rule book is available to the comprehension of your own understanding if you seek to find it. Don't let that be taken away. It's your choice to choose or to lose. Never giving up means to never stop trying. But, that is easier said than done,

because to qualify in the end, you have to get it done or die trying. My advice is known worldwide, "Just do it!"

ACKNOWLEDGMENTS

It is with great reluctance that I write these acknowledgements because so many have made me whole. I cannot mention everyone, but you know who you are. I Love You!

I acknowledge the God Source from whom I come, as does all inspiration; but foremost, I want to give thanks to my earthly Dad for always being there for me even after death. I salute you, Mr. Neahmiah Teasdell, affectionately known as "Mr. Bill".

We seldom look upon this life as having two Fathers, but my Father "Bill" is now in heaven with The Father, and that is an inexpressible love. Thanks Dad, for being the only one qualified to marry my Mom, who I also salute in life and love and for never being less than Love.

My Mom, affectionately known as Mama Bernice, Aunt Bernie, and Day Mom: She is the super duper woman of strength and southern fortitude, officially known as Willie Mae Haskell Teasdell, a real manifestation of God's power.

Then, there are my many relatives, too numerous to name, with the exception of a few: My two sisters, Pat and Lourie, shared in several of my beginning life lessons. Leonard "Moody" Haskell, the first male cousin to always make me feel I belonged, still brings tears to my eyes because of how he embraced me with his unique love of acceptance and kindness. I could never figure out how Leonard got his nickname because he was certainly far from being moody! May his soul continually rest in the peace and love of God. Moody was my first close cousin to die suddenly, and I miss him greatly.

I dearly love and acknowledge my daughters Nicole, Lakisha and Megan for their outpour of love. I give a special shout out to my Keisha, who embraced me as Daddy long before I found the courage to marry her and Megan's mom, the late Michelle Lizette Wilson-Teasdell. God rest her soul. I know that most of these poems were written because of what we shared. She made love the challenge worth fighting for.

I also cannot neglect to mention those who put the "fire under my butt" to keep stepping forward. For the inspiration of my NOW, to bring this book to printed form, is a host of Love representatives.

Dang, and if not for these special souls, I wouldn't be this far forward. The emotion of love is really swelling when I think of the energy, time and effort poured out to me by my Coach, Jo Anne Meekins of Inspired 4 U Ministries, and Rev. Valerie Love of the Destiny Coaching Academy. If not for their tenacity, this edition would still be collecting dust, like bones in a grave. Thanks for the resurrection. It is purely Divine!

Through her coaching program, "Write Your Book in 90 Days," The Rev. Valerie Love also divinely connected me to many loving souls in The Love Journey, Inc. community, facilitated by 'Lady Love' Janine Ingram.

So, a BIG THANKS for that spiritual connection, which led me to a newfound family of love soldiers: My First Lady and Earth Angel, now wife, Rev. Arlene Kahet; Min. Janine Ingram; Min. Rosah J. Hodge; James Gilmore; Rev. Mama Joy, Mama Sunshine, 'Queen Hostess' Mama Claudette Reddic, Emir J. Otto Price III, and oh so many, many more. You know who you are! Thank you all for the Love.

*"Living Thought is a
level of communication which
many know about, but don't talk about."*

INTRODUCTION

Had I not experienced it for myself, I would never have believed that words really do come out of thin air. Nor would I have imagined that "these words" could structure phrases, complete sentences and thought patterns that could be transcribed onto paper as though coming from someplace else to pass through me!

This was a 'WOW' moment that helped me better understand the importance of "scribes" during ancient times. I see how "scribes", then and now, can affect people of every land, because *"words move the soul"*.

In today's vernacular, "scribes" are known as poets, songwriters, hip hop artists, rappers, screenwriters, novelists, authors, spoken-word artist, and more because of the messages they convey to the masses. Many of them credit *inspiration* as the catalyst to their work, but there is something much deeper than they dare to share.

This collection of poetry and prose contains the spiritual transmission of *Living Thought* messages that have come through me, activated by my life experiences.

Yes, *Living Thought* is an intangible energy that connects with everyone, but not everyone is listening. This energy has existed over millenniums, beyond the confines of man's limitations. It transcends the need for wires, receivers and transponders.

Living Thought is a level of communication which many know about, but don't talk about, like when you're thinking about your favorite song and feel a "nudge" to turn the radio on, and that very song is playing. In our foolishness, we brush it off as a coincidence, but it is NOT! This is because, some way, somehow, all things are connected through frequency, vibration, or wave.

In this book, are the expressions of words that have helped me through some of my darkest and brightest moments of *"feeling and hearing something."* Now, I am able to share them with you.

There was a time I had no idea such a thing could exist, until one day I sat still and let the expression of 'thought emotion' reveal itself through pen and pad. Doing so was an alternative to punching my fist through a wall or angrily growling at the top of my lungs.

Instead, I chose to *allow* 'Living Thought' to invade my space of consciousness and express itself, even through words I did not know or thought I had never heard. This is why I included a glossary.

The crazy thing about these new found words is that they actually fit the context of the feeling expressed.

"Extraordinary Epiphanies of a King" is also a compilation of scripts found years ago, lying abandoned in the basement of my past. I couldn't just leave them there, so it is here, I compose my first gift to you. I hope you gain insight from them, as they have given comfort to me. *Living Thought,* who would have thought?

ESCHEW NOT

In a world so full of change, as we each
search for those constants in satisfaction
and peace, the enlightened discover that
which is.

What say we then, of the real, and that
which is not?

Imposters, duplicates, imitations and
assimilations, are found, exposed and
revealed for what they truly are.

Yet, if "IT" is not real, then, what be 'its'
worth when measured against stability,
consistency or the things of the infinite?

True worth is more than a measure of the
consciousness found in man;
For true worth is established beyond time
itself.

As is truth and the existence of the soul,
the transformation of energy, and
the knowledge of the unknown.

What then, shall we say of that which is real?

For, 'real' cannot be changed because it is 'the real' that cannot be stilled.

The mark of the eternal, the issuance of truth, is 'that' which never changes.
Yet, our spirituality remains eschew.

CAN YOU SAY GOODBYE TO A DEAD MAN?

How do you say goodbye to a dead man?
The one who is forever in your mind.
You know where the body is resting,
Yet memories are constantly alive.

Your thoughts of him, they linger,
And the thoughts aren't really sad;
They exist as pleasant memories,
Dancing inside your head.

I know the flesh has rotted;
It's four years past and gone.
Yet, I still can't help but visit
The place it now belongs.

Yeah, I know it is a dead man
Beneath the soiled earth;
But yet, I remember father
And the love of more than worth.

So, do say goodbye to the dead man,
For, the dead, they cannot speak.
But, maybe I'll just remember,
It's the body that wouldn't keep.

Ever notice that living, really ain't about staying! But, real living is more about figuring out that everyone is scheduled to go somewhere other than here!

ONCE WROTE

Memories of words once wrote can seldom
be found, once given the wings to fly at
random. But, random is never a word
given to fly!

For, just as a boomerang is designed,
so is the word sent and assigned;
But, its purpose ought always be divine!

Each one joined to another gives a
message within a passage.
A passage can be a way,
a message in things to say,
As memories recall what was once said.

A message that was once said,
or written, can fly away;
But words fly not away,
for space is limited.

And in time, the word returns to perch,
until its time comes to move into flight
again.

Then, somewhere, someday, sometime

along its journey of space and time,
You may have the fortune of your words
returning its good back to you.

If, of course, the words you use are used
for the good!

BEWARE OF THE VESTIBULE

Beware of the vestibule,
    Where anything can be.
Beware of the vestibule,
    That cannot dare to scream!
You ought to be more cautious
    Of the things there that you do.
There could be a trap designed
    To make you as a fool.
You'll think that it is harmless,
    When ain't nobody around,
When the little things you go to do
    Seem to only make you smile!
Well, your smile has reached its limit,
    When in the darkness you did seek,
Those little things that stimulated,
    For tomorrow you may weep,
In the vestibule.

*"You played within the vestibule of the
temptations of your life; and now you
wonder of the issues that now
brings to you your strife!"*

A LITTLE BIT OF LIFE IS NEVER ENOUGH

Life, in and of itself, is partial and not whole when separate from that which is Divine. Therefore, the deity and divinity of life constitutes much more than man can conceive. The divine nature of the true Deity of life is Love, because life without love has no true substance. Hence, life lacks its essence without the awakening of love. Therefore, the two are not twine, but thine, and of that, there can be only One.

The honest man must face the things of spiritual presence that is truth. For most who choose not to believe, believe not because they do not honestly seek out the truth of the spiritual presence in life. The reality of these conjectures surmises that *the essential creating energy force* is 'The Word.' For example: Logos – the Source of world order and intelligibility, or the self-revealing thought and will of God. The Eternal – The Continuance. LIFE – in and of itself, is not a separate being, but a separate entity of the deity co-eternal, which is not partial but a whole. Hence, our association with the All.

SHADOWS OF

Shadows of this and shadows of that,
Are not images... this makes no sense.
Understanding flees the consciousness of
mind. Frustration strangles all that's left
behind.

Existence ever changing,
as do the shadows of the mind.
Shadows ever changing,
as the sun and moon does shine.

The rays of light directly shows
the outline of what is.
The light reflecting, indirectly moves
silently through the entrances of time.

NO ONE

No one knows the pain in me,
when of myself, I'm not trying to see.
The fake one comes, then spits venom
towards me. My Master sees them
and His protection is upon 'We'.

I've never been alone,
though along the road I walk.
One foot steps, the other comes up.

Where do I go? Only the Master knows.
Where I have been only makes me grow...

Stronger each day, as each hour goes by.
My strength is of the Master, for without
Him I would fry.

But along the way,
we observe what's round about.
And yet, I'm not above myself,
nor above anyone else.

Still, no one knows the pain,
the pain within me.

I ain't about the pain;
Of this, I'm not trying to be!

The distraction of self...
the attraction of need.
Me? We? Need?
No way *that* I can see.

For, "It's weak to be a needy being,"
is what some folks may believe;
But, who are we fooling, we need is what
we be!

Yet, still I am reluctant
and not trying to believe.
I want to say that no one
has any need for me.

I want to see that I am not
a need within itself,
Yet, within myself, my spirit pleads
the need for someone else.

THE ACCUSER

We are One. We are many.
He is one --- he stands alone.
His power is fear, his hurt is dear.
He won't ever leave us alone.
He's always yelling
how we've been wronged.

The accuser is busy,
always fighting to the bone.
Attempting...
he wills to destroy God's people.
Always tempting
is his plight for a new clone.

Oops! There goes another one.
Laughter after the pain.
He's constantly consistent;
He thinks that he will reign.

The accuser is the adversary
of each and everyone;
While we run up and down the streets,
as though we're having fun.

Our pain, we're hiding.

Our tears, we're crying;
but, no one shall be aware.
For, of the things we feel inside,
we'd rather choose not to care.

No one else seemed to care,
so why the hell should we?
Oops! There goes the accuser again,
attempting to feed even me.

"Oh my God!" is my plea;
"Help me face my unbelief."

PAID ATTENTION

Eventually frustration, anger, resentment, and bitterness will overcome the ones who do not capture all they hoped for, desired and wanted to achieve in life if they make no strides toward accomplishment.

The solution is not found in not having hopes, wants, or desires for your life. The solution is found in developing the belief, cultivating healthy growth, and nurturing everything that can and will make things happen for you and around you. These must be given due attention, so that the vehicles of hopes and wants, desires and achievements will obtain the necessary fueled ingredients to move onward effectively.

What logic is it in possessing a car without any fuel, less fuel is also obtainable? What logic is it, to possess a fueled car with no path to travel or no place to travel toward? For what is it to travel with no designated destination to achieve or even to move aimlessly with no purpose?

For such actions can acquire no
accomplishments, except to have
time and fuel spent needlessly?

But, I say move or be moved,
because there is a greater picture
to the purpose of life
than just you being in it!

DONE

I'm finished, I'm toast,
I'm done, I'm a dud.
I can't stand the way
things are being done.

I'm around and can't leave.
I'm stuck and can't see.
I'm not the one I thought I'd be.
I don't exist; Yet, I can't
chase out the fear.

What do I do
to get up out of here?
I'm stabbed in the heart,
and choked by the throat.
I walk around only as
a lost and lonely ghost.

LINES

Strangled is the mind
that is running out of time
when living in a world
of two or three.

It loses sense of time
when crossing all these lines;
Confused, yet not real certain
of things to be.

The Ancient One of time
knows more than all these lines;
And answers from Him come
if you believe.

And as the time does fly
when crossing all these lines,
You'll find that peace within
begins with thee.

SHORT LIVED

Salmon, unlike Solomon,
shows wisdom nonetheless.
They know that in their lives
they must give it all their best.

Up the stream they come
while bears are on the run.
To devour is enjoyment to the bone.
Salmon when they spawn,
they know their life is done;

But not before their time,
as it is told.
Salmon, as it's known,
will grow to be as old
as salmon if their task,
they hold it bold.

FAMILY TREES

America is so beautiful
If ugly people leave;
They're the ones who
cling tightly and cleave.

Smelling up the place
with thoughts of "Hate that race,"
and no foundation as to "Why the need?"

For, there is no need to hate;
No race is second place.
Yet, quite different than another,
if you can see.

But the ugly people see
through eyes of poopy seeds;
For they can't see the poop
that's smeared within their trees.

B®OTHER

Oh, the bother,
me with no brother.
Sometimes I wonder why.

Oh the headache!
Me and my heartache;
Sometimes I cry deep inside.

But, then I discover
that I have more than a bother
If I ignore the brothers that be.

Because when I am bothered,
it's me and my brothers,
Of whom sharing of the kingdom
brings answers why,
Living can be just as sweet,
while on this side.

WORD-VERB

The spoken word,
those structured verbs,
Will now be engraved for the days...

Of reflection for some,
the revelation of One;
And for others,
a path toward this day.

CHOICES WE KEEP

I too, am one acquainted with this life.
I've walked out of pain, and back again.
I've heard the voices of many in song,
in poetry, in word.

There comes a time for all things,
And then, there comes a time for
certain things to cease, and be no more.

It's all through the choices we keep.
Some choices lead to life.
All are led to death.

But, somewhere in eternity
there will be those who
may choose to reflect
upon moments that have gone by.

But, for others, their pain of choices
will be never ending...
and peace never found.
Because of the choices of many,
there will be no voices under the ground.

SHAMEFUL LUST

Sexual orientation,
Rules and their manipulations,
Upon society at large is an issue.

People of same gender,
Making love when they render
themselves to desires unseen.

"Distasteful," they say.
"Sustained" or "Let's slay it,"
the wonders of man never cease.

But, the time shall soon come
when all under the sun
shall perish without a moment to weep!

What shall it be,
when all, who then were men,
must stand before the judgment seat?

Decisions without morals,
will then be of no quarrel
because, the rules of on high
never sleep!

The time then, will be judged,
along with the moon and the sun,
and every man that ever has been.

For, the time will have come
when the mortality of one
will be judged for the company they keep.

(*See Romans 1:18-28*)

GROWL

My awakening is resurfacing. I'm different.
I cannot ignore my intelligence,
for in doing so, I then am truly ignorant.

What nature of logic exists
to choose to be ignorant
or of the mindless?
What is it that dares take
possession to choose such?

Order does not have to have a routine!
Like a vampire that has no reflection,
is as myself when I have no desire
to reflect upon the past!

To see yourself. Not to see yourself.
To see the good. Not to see the evil.
To see the beauty. Not to seem beautiful.
The beast. Now he is loose
because he refuses to accept the evil.

But, he is both! He struggles,
as we all should...

To contain the beast within.

MILES TO GO

There's been so many miles
of pain I've traveled...
And the dust is still in my clothes.
I often try to brush it off,
and that's when it gets in my nose.

My eyes may water,
My breath may change,
A tear may come,
but I'll be okay.
For those are the miles that have been,
And I still have several miles to go.

Somewhere along the way,
I'll probably change my clothes.
Each moment, each pain,
Some were fruitful, some in vain.

But nonetheless, I shall gain
In my travel that which I must seek;
For, the miles I have traveled...
will always be mine to forever keep.

Thanks for sharing.

DARK SUNSHINE

What I have is very complicated,
but it is worth it, if it is "I" who possess it.
Therefore, it is I who have been granted
the ability to master it.

That too, has been given.
That too, only few can earn.
Those who do not have
the ability to control it,
do not have it.

Take stock in what you have—
in what you possess!
Remember, if you allow yourself
to be possessed, then
what you have belongs to
that which possesses you.

I am just one. One man of
a world full of many.
I was made to be Special,
because of my individuality.
Thus, the danger!

I have an enemy, because I am Special.

This enemy cannot stand that I am
Special, so comes my danger.

There was a time when I had chosen not
to be aware of being special anymore.
My enemy knew of a particular strategy,
and cleverly devised a plan for my
destruction. *It did not work!*

To be someone special
is everyone's desire in life.
To have someone,
or even something to love,
makes everyone feel a special need
that generates a special feeling
that most feel they cannot do without.

If you allow yourself to fall victim
to not feeling special anymore,
the enemy will devour you.

If you allow yourself to fall victim
to the addiction of the need that
can be generated of the feeling only,
then you will be as prey to anything
the enemy can conjure up against
the purpose that is "You".

If you do not hold fast in
the knowing that you are Special,
then there will be no foundation
strong enough to hold you up,
for your fall is sure to come.

Being yourself, when you are many, takes an ability to know when to be, and when not to be. It is later than you think!

For 'We' all are both of good and evil. *"The Lord made all kinds of trees grow out from the ground – trees that were pleasing to the eye, and good for food. In the middle of the garden were the tree of life and the tree of the knowledge of good and evil."* (Genesis 2:9 NIV)

Do not forget that the 'first man' ate fruit from the tree of the knowledge of good and evil. And even as written by Kahlil Gibran in The Prophet, *"And he answered: Of the good in you I can speak, but not of the evil. For what is evil but good tortured by its own hunger and thirst? Verily when good is hungry it seeks food even in dark caves, and when it thirsts it drinks even of dead waters."* You see, what you take into yourself will always have its outcome. For, it is not uncommon to hear it said, "You are what you eat!" or "Food for thought!"

No, I do my best to judge not; For, I am not yet what I ought to be. And I may very well not be what I'm supposed to be, but I exist. You see, I am one who has already traveled 60 plus years of this life and yet, I expect a very long journey still lies before me. The continuation of creation is far more than real because I know that God is not finished with me yet.

But, one thing is for certain,
and this you can take to the bank:
"I ain't what I used to be!
And that's a natural fact."

DESIRES OF THE FLESH

Desires of the flesh
are haunting nonetheless;
they wait for any moment to play.

Desires of the flesh are waiting
for a guest to manipulate and
or to sway.

Some will say, "Away"
with these desires that will play,
to twist and to dance for another day.

Others say, "Please stay
to live life and display;
whatever is your will, it'll be okay."

But, those that say "Away!"
Are more aware in many ways,
That in desires of the flesh,
Satan persuades.

HIM

God is in control, is a wonder for the soul.
His will is worth more than gold.
He'll be with you in growing old.
This is how the story is told;
For your heart shall not grow cold.
As you keep believing, it shall be
"You" amongst the bold.

It is a fool that dies in the lack
of understanding who "He" is.
It is the devil, who sets the stage,
in an attempt to prove
Our worthlessness to God.

God does not tempt us
because God knows our hearts,
and will stand on His certainty
of knowing who we are!
Do you know who God knows YOU to be?
Do you know *Who You Are?*

Just where does your devotion lie?
For in each man,
lies the desire to worship...
Something or something else!

KING TO THE KING

King of the King
Is what I was made to be,
For self-realization
Has been a struggle for me.

The knowledge of what is left
of my hidden destiny
is knowing first and foremost
that Jesus Christ is King.

I may never be always right
in the life that I live;
I can only obey,
continuing to learn how to give.

What I have of myself
is nothing you see,
Unless I realize the divinity
that lives inside of me.

This life is so full
with many uncertainties;
But, the one fact is the knowing
that all has been forgiven...

For, We own "No" thing,
and "NO ONE" owns ME.
Because I, first and foremost,
belong to the King of Kings;

And of this knowing,
EVERYTHING will come into being!
If it is the Father's will, for it all to be.

The Father of all Creation is good
and wants all good for me.
And in the knowing of this,
then all men shall be free!

But, it is only
for each of us collectively,
to choose His Holy will,
for all of this to be.

WE

Carve your path,
and make it right!
The knowing of you
is everything to me.
You know what is wrong,
so make it your fight!

You guide me, you mold me,
you fill me with ease,
to be all of what I ought to be.
In the knowing more of you,
I too shall be free.

The realization of my destiny,
Is steeped in the knowing,
You shall always be!

Eternally grateful I am to Thee,
For, in showing me the way
I am able to see,
That God is of You,
and God is of Me,
And with that knowledge...
We are Eternally We!

GOD'S GIFT

Why destroy such Royalty
When it's the mind that cannot see
The wonders of the worlds above.

A guiding light,
The truth of Love,
The heart is placed so carefully
Within the chest where none can see.
The heart and soul of all that be,
The Truth of Love Eternally.

So why destroy such Royalty
When life is just a place to see
This side alone, for just the present,
For Life itself has more to cherish.

EYE OF THE MIND

The eye of the mind
is just not what it seems.
It conceives several things
that are not to be believed.

Beyond the sense of sight,
the imagination roams...
Through those forbidden doors
that pierces your very soul.

The eye of the mind
is the one that's unseen.
It conjures up the thoughts
not found in any dream.

Yet, carefully it's triggered
to manipulate and scheme...
And plays out any game,
any name, any scene.

Beware! But, how can we?
When strategies reveal
The eye of the mind
is the playground that's unreal.

Realities untold,
imaginations unfold
The heart becomes
a vulnerable soul
that may grow cold.

Beware all ye wanderers
of these regions beyond control.
The eye of the mind sees more
than any truth, or any wish;
For, any role can be foretold.

"E" IS THE REALITY

"E" is a reality
when the tank is out of fuel.

"E" is the reality
when you find that you've been fooled.

"E" is that endurance found
when "giving in" is through!

How on Earth will we be free
when "E" is on the run?

For Eternity is infinity
of unlimited expanse,
While Destiny is just a moment...
when "E"ternity is Rest.

FREEDOM: WHAT DO YOU MAKE IT?

Compilations of emancipation.
Annihilation of an alien nation.

No one is home
when freedom cannot roam
In a land where life is perishing.

Yet, hope for the future breaks
from the recesses of the mind,
To bring renewed life
to what was left behind.

And, then again,
we search life's pages
to develop and to spark;
For life is only eternity,
beginning at the start.

MIND, BODY, AND SPIRIT

The renewing of our minds is most important. In the renewing, lies the true transformation required in the developing of our minds to attain higher spiritual acuity, wisdom and sight of the unseen.

We are developing our spiritual growth through the many expressions of the soul. The soul expresses itself through the actions of the body, and the thought energies of the mind.

There is no separation of the mind, body and spirit; Not while the manifestation of the animated living soul continues to breathe and move and have its being through the Life-Spirit that brings it.

There can be no separation which can be claimed as detached from the whole, as One. Not one of the three, can be ignored, nor rejected, outside of the time of which we must lay the body down for eternal rest.

We are One, and have been designed for specificity. Although we have many members in one body, all the members do not have the same function; So we, being many, are one body in "Spirit" and individually members of one another.

For, if we do not also stay conscious of the necessities of the body, then we shall become prey to an "imbalanced weakening" that will hinder the development of our mind and spirit as well.

Therefore it is important not to leave out the third component, just as it is important to remember the understanding of the Trinity, in the heavenly realms.

So, it is quite significant for balanced growth to stay cognitive of the earthly trinity of the mind, body and spirit, and to recognize that an unclean mind hinders the spiritual growth process of the soul.

No spiritual growth, pollutes any mental growth. Spiritual growth flows and leaves no stagnation, just as water that does not flow, would eventually become stagnant if it is not allowed to flow with the fluidity of that which keeps it alive.

The temple, which is the body, must be maintained accordingly, just as would any integral part of a beautifully flowing fountain ought be. This must be done, in order to maintain the continued beauty, strength and development of the mind and spirit to attain its higher calling beyond our moment of Now.

These accomplishments are most necessary, so that there be no breach to the foundation of the truth of living. "Well-being" is a gift of the *God Force* that brought us into existence through Love.

For, it is the weakened body that will render the entire being as prey to an unnecessary vulnerability of the mind and spirit that should not be, if not attended properly, and with loving care.

Without the appropriate considerations to the acknowledgement that the whole is one, the repercussions of neglect will leave room for weakened thoughts and the susceptibility to temptations, illness, maladjustments, and dis-ease.

Henceforth, it is important to understand that the mind, body, and spirit, in this realm are one, and should never be seen as separated, one from the other.

"But, be ye transformed by the renewing of your mind, that ye may prove what is that good, and acceptable, and perfect will of God." (Romans 12:2)

LIVING THROUGH IT

From the depths of a *Living Source* comes words into the consciousness that is transcribed into script. These are the expressions that are relayed from the inspiration of living through it all. Never being defeated; Never totally giving in; Never ever selling out that which you believe in with all your heart and soul for something of lesser value; This is living through the storm without staying in the storm.

But, as always, the struggle shall continue. That is the essence of living. Resistance is always a continuing factor as life continues within this current realm.

Just as gravity continually has a downward pull on all things in this realm, we must forever be striving toward upper heights of life. For in it, life is living, and death is merely a beginning unknown....

Where and when is much more than a matter of chance. It's our moments of choice that determine whether we win, or whether we lose. For no one can live life unto themselves.

THE IDLE MIND

What the muck, you're out of luck.
Without a job, you want to fuss!

Your plans aren't cool,
your schemes all failed!
You know the next time caught,
you'll end up in jail!

So tired of the rat race,
it seems you'll never win!
But, have you ever wondered
of the sin that you are in?

It doesn't seem to be your fault
that you always end up lost.
When you seem to go your way,
without some equal kind of pay!

Your life seems like a hustle
to do the things you do.
But, if not for the hustle,
you would become unglued.

But still, life is for the learning,
and you got to find a way.

Because life is about the choices
that you have to make each day.

So, why do you sit idle,
with nothing else to do?
Don't you know the devil
is out to work on you?

He'll catch you sitting idle
without a thing to do;
And when he does, I guarantee
he won't stop haunting you!

So, if you're sitting idle,
without a thing to do,
Always first remember
that God is watching you!

MONSTER INSIDE, MONSTER OUT

The monster inside,
presents its own fears
to the one who lives within.
It creeps, it lurks,
it makes each a jerk
of the foolish aches of sin.

Its pain, its woes,
its ignorance unfolds,
A war waged against man.

The monster invades
the consciousness
To rule the hearts of men.

The monster within
is hard to behold;
It disguises itself
and then lashes out bold.

Odd feelings within,
become disgusting as sin,
to make the warmest
of hearts grow cold.

The pain is not true,
But really only a tool
to manipulate the ones
in 'Sinner' School.

The monster is cruel
and carries no rules;
He's there to destroy
and take away all joy.

So you best be aware
when you think you don't care,
for the monster is waiting each day...

To tear us to threads,
when we're unaware,
for the monster within
wants to stay.

WE ARE MORE

As I go through this life observing bodies
of those who are deceased,
It's amazing to realize
that not one of them can speak.

The amazement is not
that the dead cannot speak,
It's that at one point in time
they had voice...

We are far more than we thought
inside that drives the thing that should;
That something gives forth
the strongest inclination
of the power of life that could.

Yet, what is this source of inclination?
My God! Let's not be shy!

More than the physical, a force unknown,
That cannot be touched or seen of the eye.
But only with the eye, of the living life
force, that is found in the 'You' and the 'I'.

SHE

The female deserves respect from being the entity that becomes "She" all by itself, of herself, by the creation that she is, and is to become.

Hence, any man who does not recognize the beauty of this creation of the Creator, has yet to mature, to become what he ought to already have been. From the basic premise of wrongly equating his manhood, and being a man as one in the same, he falls short; and his ignorance is thus twofold.

Of this premise, it can be reasoned that any male entity, who has yet, no respect for the female entity, has yet to mature, or evolve to the level of being truly a real man. But he has degraded his own self to be less, instead of allowing himself to become the more. For what is a man who is, but a hindrance to all others, and have nothing within him to bring lift to another?

Therefore, the male can never 'judge' the female on the basis of how "She" sees herself.

In essence, the male can never be in position to judge, for he is not her God. No matter what her position in life may be! For "She" may not have matured to know the fullness of her own self-worth.

There is only One Creator, all else would merely be assistants to the One...

All that honor "Creation" must acknowledge their part within it. For not one, can exempt themselves from the needs of her soul!

For, always instilled within her, is the knowing of a special gift of heaven that is germinating to be the True Essence of She!

POET'S TREE

I find escape in poetry,
A moment away from strife.
I find escape in poetry,
A moment revealed of life.

The pain is transferred,
from the mind into pen.
The ink, then turns
the minds and hearts of men.

The brain translates the frames
of that which was insane;
And the truth flows to release
only some of the pain.

The words transform
what once was said
of that needed stay of ecstasy,
Which once escaped reality.

We ponder thoughts that make no sense,
in this world we live, that has no fence.
Revealing life, through pen and thought,
Is often termed a work of "Art".

THE FALLING OF THE LEAVES

Travelers, we are through time and space.
We see. We hear. We touch.
As the seasons have air,
and the air we do share,
With the created things that be.

Look at the trees and their leaves,
as autumn does come.
The colors so arrayed,
until the leaves begin to fall...

There's diversity of beauty
in each and every land,
Giving hues of red, green,
orange and tan.

When there was a time,
that they all had a rhyme,
Of green in varying shades,
throughout the countryside.

Now, as the season has changed,
and the leaves are now fallen;
All have turned to brown,
except the ones that are calling *Out,*

that life has so much more to give.

Can't you see the evergreen,
with that forever flow?
Yet all the shades of yellow,
orange, tan and red...
Have left the trees, as does the
purpose of living continues
to move onward.

For, even the bare bark,
now lays exposed;
as the many colored foliage
All come together as one,
once again.

But, in looking very carefully,
amongst the many trees that be,
There are those, whose bark
lies very differently.

So that all else may come;
so that all else may see...
And this is the story
of the falling of the leaves.

REJECTION

I'm so very tired of rejection,
It really, really makes me sick!
I wanted a Coca-Cola,
some chips and other hits;
But, I am at the PX,
and the "I.D." I have ain't it!
So, I turn away in anguish,
without the things I came to get.

It's a simple little issue,
but the pain swells up inside;
Because I'm still not healed
of the rejection I try to hide.

I write my words of anguish
to release the nagging blow;
Because it ain't about the chips,
it's about the aching in my soul!

I know, one day, it's true
that I'll recover soon.
But, only God knows what happened
to that person I once knew.

He'll be back, there is no doubt,

But I sure as hell, can do without...

REJECTION!

LET THERE BE PEACE

The way of the world, so as it is told
When it was Love, and not war,
In days of long ago.

Now, "Somebody's" feelings hurt,
But how really real is that?
Compared to a bullet
that has been struck in the back
Of an unsuspecting stranger,
Or a soldier gone to war?

The way of the world
Is the Pain within our Souls.
With pain in our souls,
As we journey through each land,
To seek a new foundation
Of a 'River' free from sand.

The sand? You do say,
Can get between your toes...
But, what about the sand
That's tossed before the blows?

There they go again,
fighting like cats and dogs...

When the fighting never stops,
Cause it's a war against our souls.

So then, the real true question is...

"What are we fighting for?"
When deep inside, our inner being,
Is a desire for PEACE,
Not war.

MAYBE LOVE

Maybe love is a ghost,
that is selective at most,
As to where, and who
she hangs out with.

Maybe, if we are not found
to have the appropriate
Character for love to accept us, then...

Maybe it is we,
who are unable to attain
to greater Levels with love.

Maybe, it is we,
who are not found to be
as receptive, as we ought to be
when love does call.

Maybe, just maybe,
forgiveness is a place,
more than merely a thing we do.

Maybe,
forgiveness is the place
Love loves most to be.

 Can you stay in the place
called forgiveness? Or,
is it you, who is always leaving???

Maybe, it is love
that finds that it is You,
Who is always leaving
the place she loves most...
and then, finds You are the deserter.

How can we be free in freedom, without
love?

If only, love could dominate all things...
I mean Real Love!

Then, wouldn't all things be Beautiful?
Because then, it couldn't be anything
else...

But, Beauty and Love!

MONKEY ON YOUR BACK

You say, "There is a monkey."
And he's strapped there on your back!

The monkey, he ain't working,
And his knowledge of things is whack.

You got nerve to pay attention,
to what the monkey say...

But the monkey ain't got
all of his senses, anyway!

Yet, there you sit a listening,
To what the monkey say!

Now, tell me really,
What in the hell...

Is your monkey for today?

DON'T LET THE DEVIL DRIVE

Okay, we got places to go;
We all are on the run.
Our mode of transportation
Is driving, minus the gun.

We now feel unprotected,
In need of any friend.
So, we pick up the hitchhiker
That seems minus the sin.

He talks a good game.
He seems just like you.
He talks of all the things
that he thinks that he can do.

He claims to be the craftsmen
of every little thing.
He's trying to convince you
of all he has to say!

You're driving down the byways,
with a destination unbeknown.
The guy sitting beside you,
thinks that he's a pro...

Of every little thing
that he keeps talking about.
Now he wants to do the driving,
and you're concerned because he pouts?

Remember, this is your vehicle;
And it is in your care.
Remember, it is the hitchhiker,
Who is paying with no fare.

Now, he's driving you...
Up the secret wall,
Talking bout he's got a mission
While he is on the run...
And it is you, Who has no idea
Of what he's running from!

You really haven't any clue
of what he's bout to do.
But this one is the hitchhiker,
who makes you come unglued.

He is not your friend!
And to cite your unawares.
This one is the devil
of all the things you dread.

You best have total recall
of what prophecy was said...
When you walked along the dream world
of the shadows in your head.

The devil is in your business.

He wants to make you run!
He'll take hold of your steering wheel
just to have his fun.

He's cunning, that's for certain!
He's wanting just to drive.
But remember, this most important thing,
He wants for you to die.

A SPARK

As a transitive verb, the word "spark" means the following:
1) To set in motion; activate; ignite.
2) To rouse to action.

At the "Beginning of Life," it is truly believed that there was "a spark," that started the whole purpose of living into action. In the middle of life, is the need for things to be set in motion, so as not to cease the movement needed for living. And at the "End of Life," we all wonder if there will be the need of any spark at all.

The End of Life! What are we waiting for? Some say, "Death" and others say, "To get into heaven". Well, each and every one of us was created for something or another. Each and every one of us is some sort of "spark" of some kind or another.

What if it was "Jesus," the real "Son of God," who was waiting for us?

What if it was "Yeshua," waiting to see us 'face to face'?

What would you have to say if He asked, "Did you do your homework?"

Whether it was right or wrong wouldn't matter, only your answer, in the time of which there is 'no time' to do, 'no more' than answer "Yes" or "No."

We are that Spark! But, of that 'spark'...
What did we do with it? What are we doing with it? What are we to do?

What sense of shame or guilt comes in the saying, "Oh, I didn't get to it in time!" or "I don't know what happened!" Or is there any sense of feeling at all? What would it really feel like in the saying, "Oh, I think the dog ate it!"?

Of the latter, I would really hope you took into account the reverse spelling of dog, because there probably won't be any other explanation that will explain what had happened to you, that consumed you!

The reverse spelling of dog is god! Yes, god with a small "g". A small "g" god that had consumed all your time, all your life, all your energy, all of you!

Ever wondered what it is like to be totally consumed?

There would be nothing left of you once completely consumed. NOTHING of You!

Have you looked into what the word "None" would do?

"Got none. Be none!" Now, that's done 'NONE' of your homework!

No Spark at all!

COME FORTH

Come forth into the light.
What makes you so afraid?
It's not your true nature anyway.

Come forth into the light,
And you will feel the many rays
Of the beauty, in the living of the day.

So what! You feel the scum
Of the deeds that you have done,
Within the darkness of the regions of the
cave.

So what! You feel ashamed
Of the games you used to play.
Remember, it was the game
that played you anyway.

So, come forth into the light.
Please try with all your might.
You'll find that there's delight
In an attempt to do what's right;
If you would only...
Come forth into the Light
Of Love!

ROLLED AWAY FROM THE TOMB

I think of the conditions we find humanity,
From those who live and walk among us,
Dead of hope and dead to the Spirit
within.

Then, I think of a man who laid dead,
Decaying in a tomb, whose name was
Lazarus. Yet, because of LOVE, he was
called forth from the grave to live again!

Many are trapped by so many negative
things of life, until they feel dead, and
cannot see no way out.

They are trapped in addictions and
wayward thinking that would lead them
to imprisonment or death:

Yet, there is life still within them to live,
but they are blinded in captivity.

They only need to see the positive
"addition" they would become to the
whole, when the "C" in addiction is
removed, and placed out of their way.

Just taking the "C" from the word
"addiction," really makes the change
to "addition," a beautiful, positive reality;
Just as a stone is rolled away from the
tomb...

Oh, by the way, the "C" is Captivity.

RESURRECTION

The Essence of the Resurrection
Is the power of Love, the power of God.
And of this, it is known that God is Love,
For only the essence of His love never dies.

Although, of our human consciousness,
Love is thought to die.
Yet, Love is also known to live!
And, of this Living Love,
True life is discovered,
Being more profound
than the human mind
Can possibly hope to imagine.

Yet, with the limitations of our intellect,
We cannot yet conceive
The whole story.

Without the right parts,
We shall nowhere come
To the realization of what the Whole
Could possibly conceive to become!
That's why so many live in...
The "not to be."

But, "The Word"
is like a two-edged sword;
And, the sword is pulled
from the Stone of revealed knowledge.
And, "The Sword"
is preparing for its Work!

I WANT TO BE

God wants all people to change
their hearts and minds,
To be inclined to Thine!

What a way to start our days,
When we begin to listen
to what He says!

The changing of that which is,
Into something that's supposed to be!
To be, to be, what it's supposed to be.

Yet, what of 'the not to be' that is?
Is not its being "to be"?
Or, is it needed to see the difference
Of that which is to be?

To be, to be, which is supposed to be?
To be, is not the now,
But what is supposed to be!

The future is the change,
The future is for the better.
The change is for the better,
Or the change is for the worst.

The change is for the hearts and minds
Of those who know the verse...
"For, the Stone and the Sword
Are preparing for its Work!"

LISTEN...

Your preference should matter;
And of the right mental attitude,
We all should want the better.

But, if you are one who chooses the worst
And of you, there is a burning desire to
Have what is not only worse, but that
which only continues to get worst!

Then, should you not first check
the condition of your mind's rationale?

For if the worse is what you seek to
obtain, then be mindful that a greater
negativity of change will someday come;

And you will then discover
that "To Be" Is something;
And, "not to be"
Is no existence at all!

What once was yours
is now reported stolen!
We now know where it was put...
Just slightly out of your reach.

Well, that which is yours belongs NOT to the one who stole it! So, what do you do?

Sometimes you have to go and get what's yours to have! There will be a struggle, because you weren't supposed to find it. At least, so as the thief would believe.

Yet, it is told that possession is nine tenths of the law.

Could this be right? But, not right for you?

So what do you do?

> *"And from the days of John the Baptist until now, the kingdom of heaven suffers violence, and the violent take it by force."*
> (Matthew 11:12)

GLOSSARY

Addiction: To devote or give oneself habitually or compulsively; one given over to something or another as a slave.

Annihilation: The act or process of destroying completely; wipe out; reduce to nonexistence.

Assimilate: To make similar; cause to assume a resemblance.

Being: Existence; a state of existence; a condition of particular existence.

Cleave: (2) To adhere, cling, or stick fast; to be faithful.

Compilation: The act of putting together or collecting from several sources.

Conjunctures: (1) A combination of circumstances or events. (2) a critical set of circumstances; crisis.

Conjure: (1) To call upon or entreat solemnly, especially by an oath. (2) To summon (a devil or spirit) by oath or magic spell.

Deity: A God or Goddess.

Deserter: (2) To forsake one's duty; to leave; abandon.

Dis-ease: The imbalance felt within the human species that is believed to be the catalyst for the onset of illnesses and diseases.

Divinity: The state or quality of being divine; especially the state of being a deity.

Dud: (2) Someone, or something disappointingly ineffective or unsuccessful.

Entity: (1) The fact of existence; being. (2) Something that exists independently, not relative to other things.

Eschew: Deliberately avoid using; to abstain or keep from; shun.

Expanse: A wide or open extent, as of land, sky or water.

Famuli: Plural form of Latin famulus — an attendant or servant, especially of a medieval sorcerer or archaic scholar/teacher.

Farce: Something ludicrous; an empty show; mockery.

Glimmer: A dim or intermittent light; a flicker.

Idle: (1) Not employed; inactive; lazy, shiftless (2) Avoiding employment; to pass time without purpose.

Inclination: Something for which one has a preference or leaning.

Integral: Essential for completion; necessary to the whole; constituent.

Logos: Cosmic reason, affirmed in ancient Greek philosophy as the source of world order and intelligibility. (2) The self-revealing thought and will of God, often associated with the second person of the Trinity. [Greek logos, speech, word, reason].

Maat or Ma'at: Refers to the ancient Egyptian concepts of truth, balance, order, harmony, law, morality, and justice.

Module: A self contained assembly of components that perform a specific task or class of tasks in support of the major function of a larger specified unit.

Muck: A moist, sticky mixture, especially of mud and filth.

None: (1) No one; not one; no body. (2) Not any; no part; nothing.

Perceiving: (1) To become aware of directly through any of the senses; especially to see or hear. (2) To take notice of; observe; detect. (3) To become aware of in one's mind; achieve understanding of; apprehend.

Premise: A proposition upon which an argument is based or from which a conclusion is drawn.

Resurrection: A rising from the dead; or a returning to life, practice, notice, or use; rebirth.

Spark: (n) –
1. An incandescent particle, especially:
    a) One thrown off from a burning substance.
    b) One resulting from friction.
    c) One remaining in an otherwise extinguished fire; an ember.
2. A glistening particle of something, as metal.
3. A sudden flash.
    a) A flash of light; especially, a flash produced by electric discharge.
    b) A short pulse or flow of electric current.
4. A trace or suggestion, as:
    a) A quality or feeling with latent potential; seed; a spark of genius.

b) A vital, animating factor or activating factor: the spark of revolt.

Stagnant: Foul from standing still; polluted; stale.

Stagnate: To be, or become stagnant (not moving or flowing; without a current; motionless). (2) To lie inactive; fail to progress or develop.

Surmise: To infer something without sufficiently conclusive evidence.

Trinity: (1) The state or condition of being three. (2) Any three parts of union; a triad. Also called a trinity. (3) The union of three divine figures, the Father, the Son, and Holy Ghost, in one Godhead.

Vestibule: (1) A small entrance hall or antechamber between two doors of a house or building. (3) Any cavity, chamber, or channel that serves as an approach or entrance to another cavity (opening).

I am a poet, and I didn't know it, until it was revealed by unexpected happenstance!

ABOUT THE AUTHOR

I am "B'more," born and raised, the anomaly with deep southern roots, born to answer questions. I lived a life seeking answers. I was born as the middle child between two sisters and I found myself to be the nuisance and the protector at the same time. I always seemed to be holding the throne as if I was the eldest child, but I always remained respectful to my older sister, who is 21 months my senior.

I was designed not to see things as others do. This gave me the gift that one of my dearest friends Eraka, calls "alternate sight." Please, let me explain; Prior to the birth of my younger sister, five years my junior, my older sister and I would obediently sit and watch the night sky. My Mom overheard my sister ask, "I wonder what happened to all those stars that used to be out here?" Mom knew that behind the silence of my delayed response, I was pensive in thought, as the wheels turned in my head.

I excitedly broke the silence proclaiming, "I know why the stars aren't out there like before! It's because the moon ate them up!" Full moon, less stars, my Mom cried with laughter!

As a lover of science and discovery, I would wander away from the crowd, just to explore on my own. The irony is that although people would often have to come find me, I wouldn't be lost. I just stayed away longer than expected. My Mom loves telling of my disappearance at the age of two, determined to meet my Dad at his workplace, but ended up coming home with a police cap on my head and a wad of chewing gum in my mouth, happy as a child in a candy store.

In the eighth grade, my greatest aspiration was to become a thoracic surgeon because helping people has always been my life's calling, even though I also loved drawing pictures of people and celebrities. But, drawing was a place of joy that I did not want taken away by it being demanded of me.

During my high school years, I enjoyed my work as a laboratory animal technician's assistant until I was whisked away by the beautiful Midwest campus of Earlham College. I permanently returned to Baltimore after 3 years and became a Certified Cardiac Rescue Technician for the Baltimore City Fire Department; after which, I became a full-fledged Advanced Life Support Paramedic, where I really began to discover the meaning of life unexpected.

My poetry was spawned through the pains of others, in conjunction with the pain of a relationship that led to divorce. But somehow, I always felt that writing was bound to my soul. During my college years, I just called these writings "notes" from lessons learned. In the Liberal Arts college curriculum, Humanities was a must, and it was there I became more familiar with word and art.

Pain has a strange way of squeezing the juice out of you. After Dad died, I sat in my mother's basement for hours reading words from notes I had written to ease my pain, as the explanations of "why" came to console me over the years gone by.

I had no idea of what had occurred, and had formed of itself, by itself. I was most astounded by what I had found, because I hadn't planned on reading in the privacy of the dungeon; but, my plans are always second fiddle when it comes to the will of God... Always!

I am a poet, and I didn't know it, until it was revealed by unexpected happenstance!

This work is work I do, as unto him who has bestowed the *'Talent'* that transcribes inspiration into Words. I receive this inspiration as though tuned into a radio signal, like an electronic receiver accepting a transmission.

This gift of 'Written Word' surprised even me, when I discovered my uncanny ability to seemingly capture words out of thin air, as composed within the arrangement of this book.

I find it ironic that for decades, man could not fathom the possibility of messages out of the air without wires, cables or cords. Yet, as I look around me today, I see personal wireless communication devices, receiving transmissions from nearly everywhere imaginable.

This only goes to show how imitation truly is the greatest form of flattery because 'the Learned' know that nothing can exist without first being conceived within.

We are so likened to the Creator, we desire to be as He is. But, God is far more advanced than even the highest thought that man could possibly contrive, separated from infinite intelligence alone.

Imagine, what man could accomplish when truly in unity with the Divine. Wow! First there is the unseen, then that which is seen in the visible physical realm.

With the 'Power of Choice,' we can choose to accept the things that God has for us or, we can choose not to accept the things of God, and instead, grab for something else. Shouldn't we all prefer the better of the choices that are available to each of us? However, you know there exist forces, persons, and things that prefer we have no choice at all.

Now, consider how technology has advanced from the telegraph to the cell phone, seemingly eliminating the "Paul Revere" experience. Yet, in some small way, deep down inside of me, I ponder the urgency that came upon the "Minute Men," like Paul Revere, and the importance of the messages they felt obligated to deliver. I think of their zeal and that adrenaline rush, especially when the enemy tried to sneak up on the seemingly unaware.

It is just as important today that we be forewarned of the coming of the unseen enemy, so that we can be prepared to withstand any attack with the right mental attitude and fortitude. The time has come upon us when the adversary can no longer conceal himself in deceit, and we cannot act as if the enemy is not there. The unseen will eventually reveal itself.

The lawlessness of irrational humanity has constructed this newest assault against Love and Divine power. What will be the newest delivery of *messages* that is best used to express these concerns? And what will be the best mode of communication for these messages to be appropriately heard, received, and perceived? I wonder.

"But words are things, and a small drop of ink falling like dew upon a thought, produces that which makes thousands, perhaps millions, think.

– George Gordon, Lord Byron

www.ingramcontent.com/pod-product-compliance
Lightning Source LLC
Chambersburg PA
CBHW072023040426
42447CB00009B/1709